How it is made

Maps

Text   John Baynes
Design   Robert Wheeler

Contents

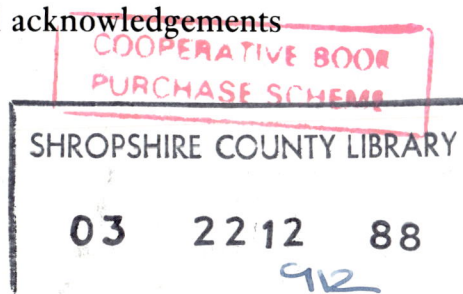

ff
faber and faber in association with Threshold Books

All kinds of maps

A map is a drawing or plan of the world in and on which we live. It may be a fairly uncomplicated map of the world as a whole, or a minutely detailed plan of a tiny part of the world.

One of the easiest ways of understanding the shape of the earth and the environment around us is to see it from an aeroplane. As well as natural features such as lakes, rivers, mountains and forests, you can pick out roads, streets and buildings such as factories. But you can't see all the details.

Maps provide this bird's eye view, with the added advantage of being able to pinpoint all the necessary details and to leave out the superfluous ones. On a grand scale, they help to present general information about the country that we live in – its towns, cities and other features; about other countries; and about the continents of which these countries form part. On a small scale, they provide essential details which help people in their work and in their leisure. A long-distance truck driver, for example, needs to see highways, main roads, garages and parking places. A walker wants to see the footpaths which he can take. Someone going on holiday will want to know about camping sites, beaches, picnic places and leisure parks.

All kinds of maps are made to fulfil these needs, and a great deal of thought and effort goes into their preparation and design. Roads are shown in different colours, according to their importance, from highway to country lane. Buildings are shown by **conventional signs**. To locate important centres, such as city halls and historic houses, names and descriptions are added. Woodlands are coloured green, rivers and lakes blue, to make them stand out and easy to recognize.

Of the many people involved in the making of a map, the three main groups are the *surveyors*, who measure and record facts about everything on the earth's surface; the *cartographers*, or map draughtsmen who interpret the information provided by the surveyors and prepare finished designs and drawings; and the *printers*, who accurately reproduce the artwork in many colours.

Topographical maps, showing natural and physical features, are produced by most countries. Many are produced by governments rather than by private companies: in England, for example, by the Ordnance Survey, in the United States by the US Geological Survey, in France by the Institut Géographique National.

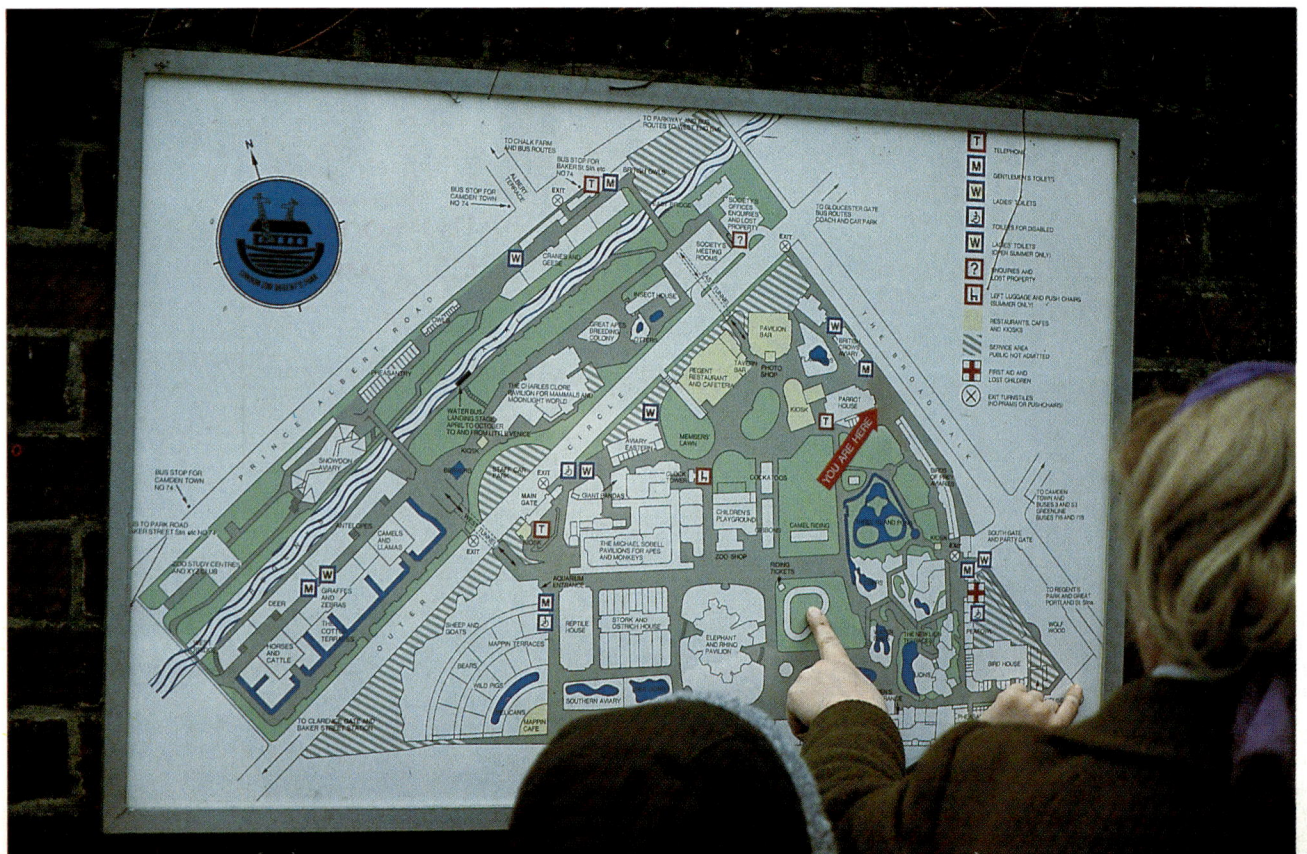

Maps, such as this one at London Zoo, help people to find their way around.

On this plan of central Manhattan, New York, the buildings have been drawn in great detail. The streets have been widened and the building heights exaggerated to make the plan easy to follow. The artist has used aerial photographs as reference. Designed for tourists, this map would not be suitable for city-planners, as some of the details are obscured behind buildings.

All the stations in the subway system are shown on this simplified schematic map. The directions and positions of the lines are purely diagrammatic, but the stations are in their correct order and the routes have been colour coded for easy reference.

Here is a selection of different maps made for a wide range of activities and interests. See how many kinds of maps you yourself can find.

The spaceman's view

The best representation of the earth is a globe, on which countries can be shown in their true position and at their same relative sizes. Distances, areas and directions can also be measured accurately. This simple but effective method of **cartography**, or mapmaking, has been used for centuries, and sailors once used globes to navigate their ships around the world.

A grid of lines can be drawn on a globe. Lines joining the two poles together from North to South are **lines of longitude**, or meridians. The line passing through Greenwich near London is known as the Greenwich Meridian. Lines of longitude are numbered in degrees East and West of the Greenwich Meridian. 180°East and 180° West make up the full circle.

Lines drawn round the globe from East to West are **lines of latitude** or parallels. The line round the centre, equidistant from the poles, is the **equator**. Lines of latitude are numbered North to South from the equator: 0°to 90°to the North Pole and 0°to 90°to the South Pole.

The problem with a globe is that it is cumbersome and cannot easily be carried around or stored. Neither is it easy to measure with a ruler. The early mapmakers, therefore, found it more practical to transfer the information on to sheets of paper, thus presenting the world as if it were flat.

This view from outer space shows the earth spinning on its axis. By comparing it with a globe, can you identify the countries?

A globe shows the true position and shape of the countries of the world.

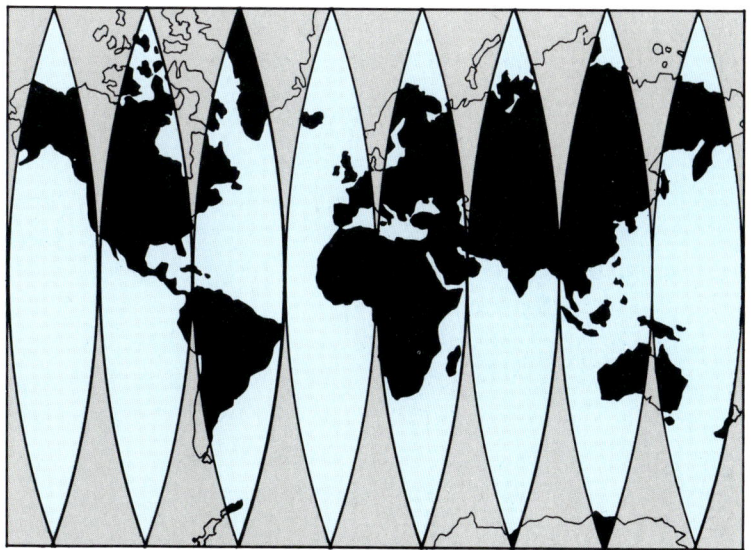

North pole

latitude

longitude

South pole

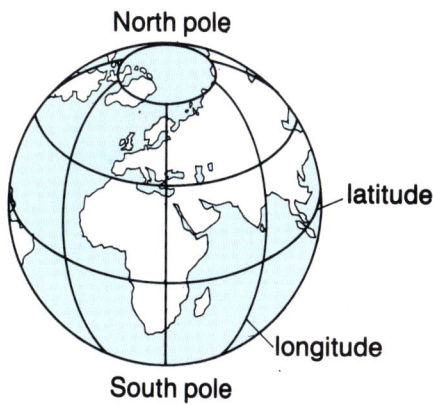

Right: Mercator produced a rectangular map of the world. The shaded areas near the North and South Poles have been stretched. Other projections are shown below.

Mercator's projection, the grey-tinted area is stretched

Stereographic projection

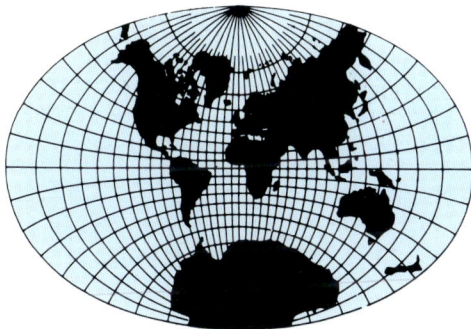

Goode's interrupted projection

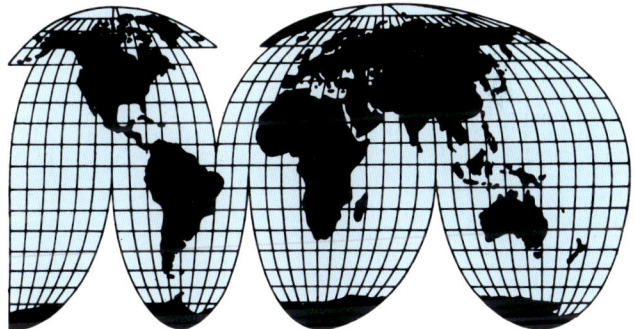

Imagine that the globe were a hollow rubber ball, which could be cut up and pressed flat on to a sheet of paper. This would be called **projecting** the globe on to the flat surface.

There are many ways of cutting a globe. It could be cut along the lines of longitude, opened out, and the areas at the north and south edges could be stretched into the shape of a rectangle. Or you could cut round the land and distort the sea areas until they were flat.

The many different ways of presenting the curved surface of the globe on a flat piece of paper all involve 'stretching' or 'shrinking' part of the globe. Different projections have their advantages and disadvantages; none is perfect. On some projections the shape and areas of the countries are retained; on some, directions can be measured accurately, and so on.

When mapping a small area such as a field or a parking lot, the earth's curvature is not visible, so a projection will not be necessary. Maps of larger areas, however, will need a projection.

Look at the maps in your atlas and see what projections have been used.

The compass

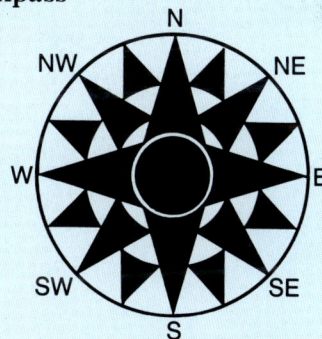

The face of the compass shows the directions North, East, South and West, and is further divided into intermediate points. The magnetized needle on the compass points roughly towards the North Pole and provides a convenient method of finding your bearing in relationship to the pole. Navigators can use these compass points to plan their journeys.

There is a small variation between the direction of **magnetic North** shown by the compass and the direction of true North (the North Pole). This variation is usually described on the margin of the map.

Choosing a map scale

The amount of detail printed on a map depends on the size of the paper and the **scale** of the map. Scale is achieved by reducing the size of a real feature or object (e.g. a mountain or a building) to its relative size on a map or a plan.

If you draw round your hand you will produce a plan at life size. There is no reduction, so the scale is 1:1. If the length of the drawing is reduced by half, the scale is 1:2. Reduced by one quarter, the scale is 1:4, etc. You could go on reducing it and drawing it at many different scales.

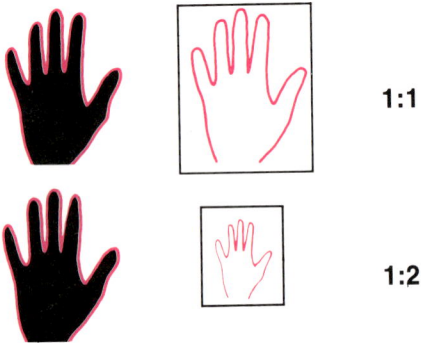

With an object as large as a building, the plan or map would be reduced many more times: for example at a scale of 1:100.

There is a simple relationship between measurements taken on the map and measurements on the building. One centimetre measured on the map would represent 100cm (or 1 metre) on the building. This is very convenient, because any measurement taken on the map can be multiplied by 100 to provide the measurement on the building.

When one unit measured on the map represents 100 units measured on the ground, the scale is 1:100. This is called the **representative fraction**. The scale of a map is usually expressed as a representative fraction or as a ratio of measurements: for example 1 inch to 1 mile.

Maps can be designed at various scales according to their use. On large-scale maps the houses are large, on small-scale maps they are small. Look at these examples.

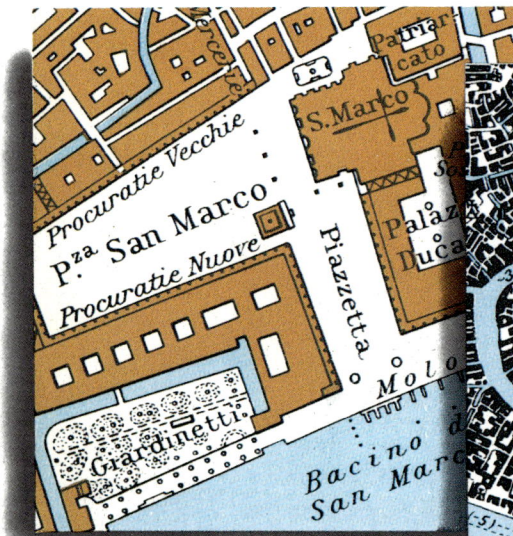

1:1

1:2

scale 1:5000
ratio   1cm = 50m

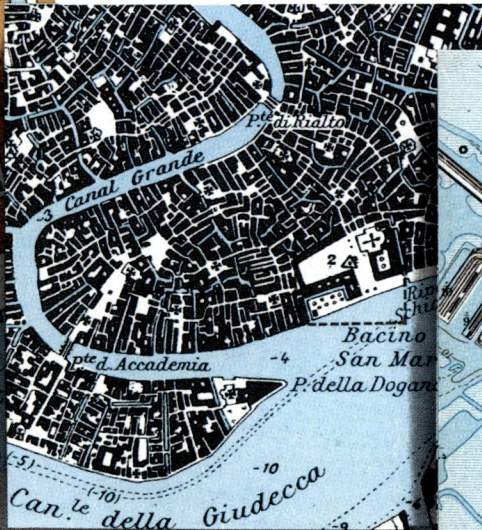

scale 1:25000
ratio   1cm = 250m

scale 1:100,000
ratio   1cm = 1Km

The choice of map scale depends on the area you want to cover and the amount of detail you expect to find on the map.
A 1:5000 scale map (in this case of Venice) can be used for exploring a city. For planning a long journey a 1:500,000 scale would be needed.

measuring distances

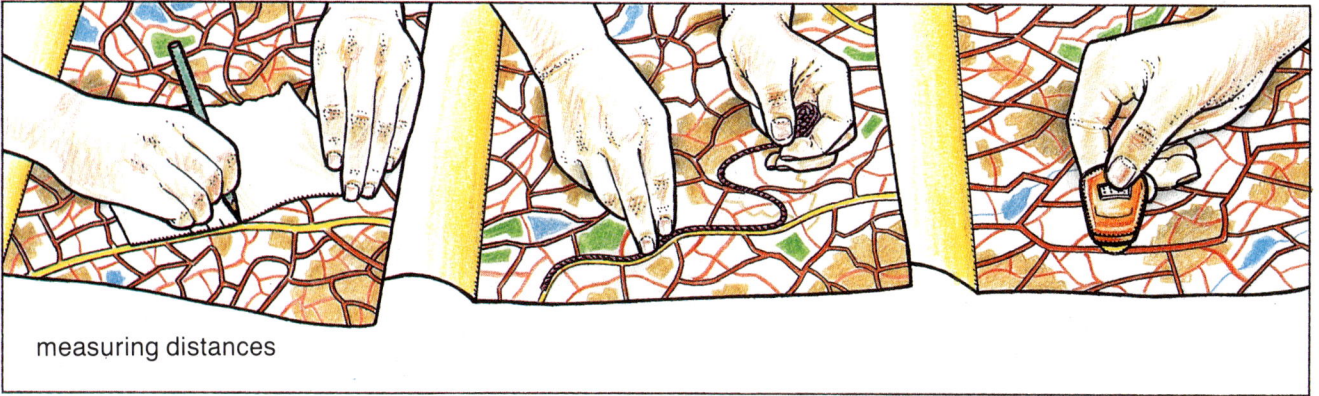

It is important to choose the right scale of map for the particular activity you intend to pursue. A good scale of map for exploring the countryside on foot, by bicycle, or by car is the 1:50,000, which shows all the roads, towns and villages in an area.

Most maps have the scale marked clearly in the margin, and there is often a **double-diced scale** showing the divisions which represent various distances.

The double-diced scale can be used to compare distances measured in different units.

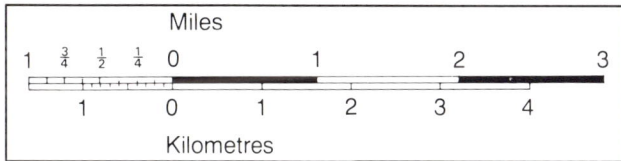

You can practise measuring distances on various scales of maps. Direct distances can be measured with a ruler. Distances along winding roads can be measured using the edge of a piece of paper, a piece of string, or a special measuring wheel.

Some maps show the distances between important points marked with a special symbol or pointer.

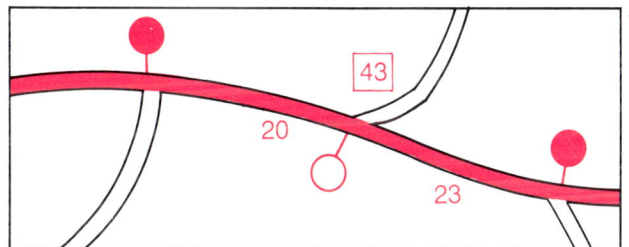

scale 1:500 000
ratio   1cm = 5Km

scale 1:2 000 000
ratio   1cm = 20Km

scale 1:12 000 000
ratio   1cm = 120Km

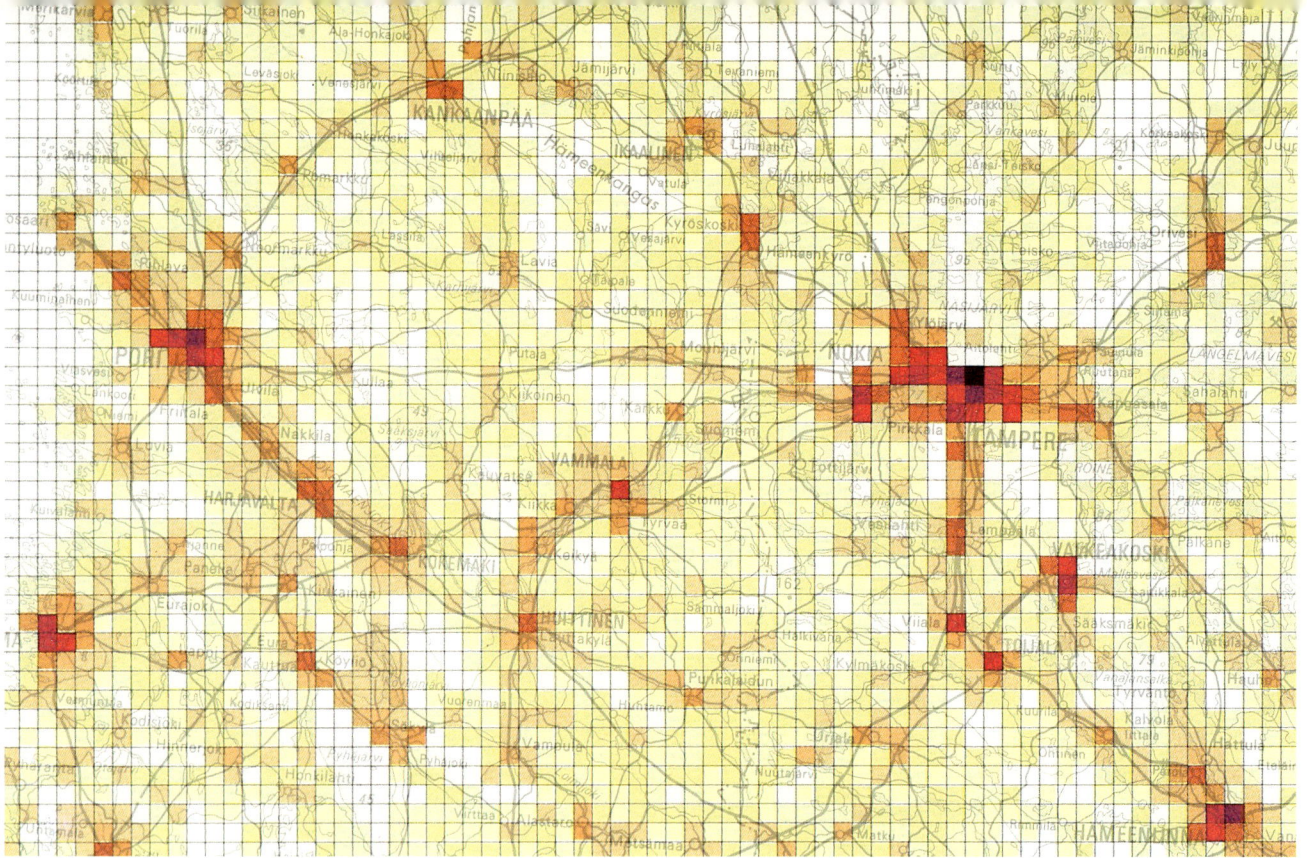

This map shows density of population with the use of different colours. The darker the area, the more densely it is populated.

Working maps

A large-scale map on which everything is true to scale is called a plan.

Make a plan of your bedroom, your kitchen, or your classroom. Draw it as if you were looking directly down upon it. Measure the length and breadth of the room, and work out the largest scale that will fit the paper on which you are drawing it. Draw in the windows, the doors and the furniture. This plan could be used for redesigning the room, so calculate, for example, how much carpet you need to cover the floor.

Architects always draw plans of a building which they are designing. On the plans they visualize the areas in which the rooms will be situated. By measuring the plan in detail, an architect can tell the builder, for example, how many bricks will be required and how much wood he will need.

A civil engineer constructing a road will use large-scale plans to decide where the road will go. He can work out where the road will have to be cut through a hillside or bridged over valleys. Geological maps show the engineer what type of rocks or soils will be found along the route, and where the nearest supply of sand and gravel can be found.

Meteorologists use maps to plot the weather, recording the temperature, pressure and wind direction. Other maps show distribution of population, vegetation, and annual rainfall.

These are examples of working maps. If you want to be an architect, a civil engineer or a meteorologist you will need to understand how maps are made, and what they signify.

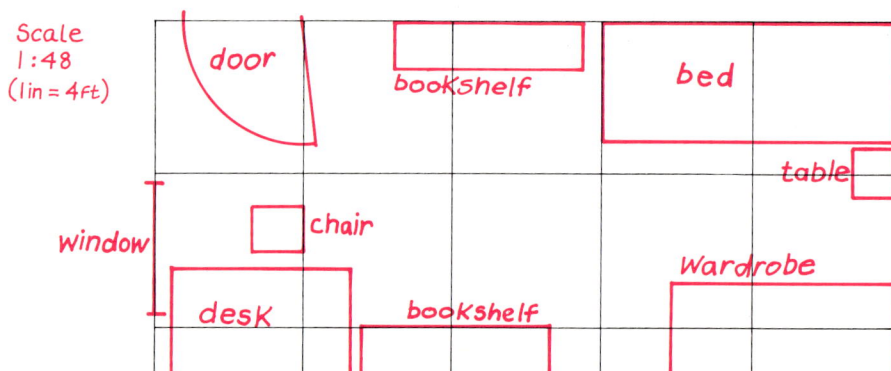

Scale
1:48
(1 in = 4 ft)

door

bookshelf

bed

table

window

chair

desk

bookshelf

Wardrobe

On the flight decks of aircraft, navigation charts are used to pinpoint the signal beacons on the ground and to determine altitude. The radar and radio stations enable the navigator to follow the correct flight paths, carefully avoiding other air traffic. Air safety depends on the accuracy of these charts.

A long distance bus or truck driver needs to know the towns and cities on his route, the route numbers, where other roads branch off, and the distances between points. These are shown clearly in simplified form on this schematic highway map.

Engineers and scientists use geological maps to study the earth, locating valuable ores and other natural resources such as oil and gas. Colour coded maps, such as this geological map, are an efficient way of providing the information.

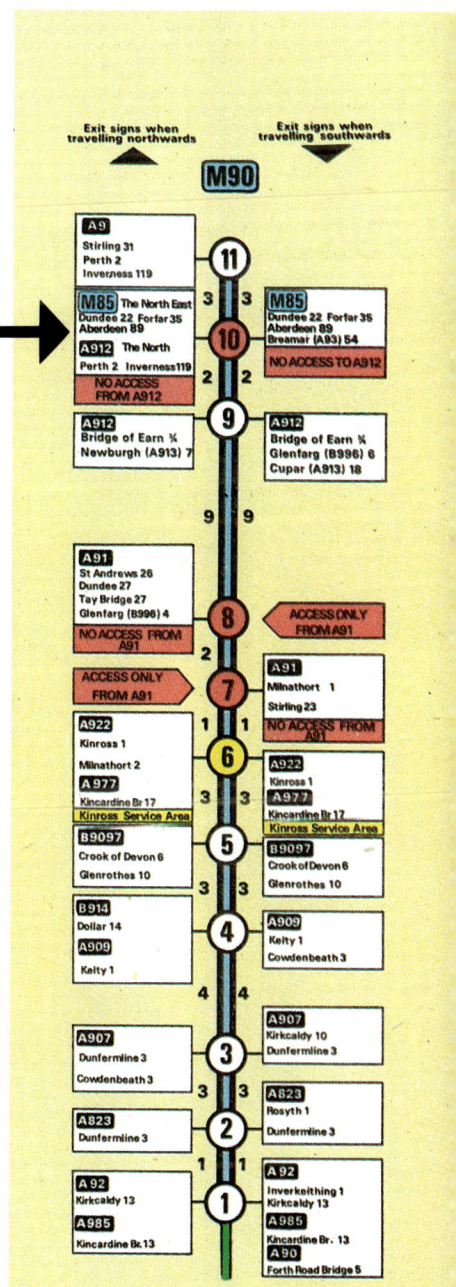

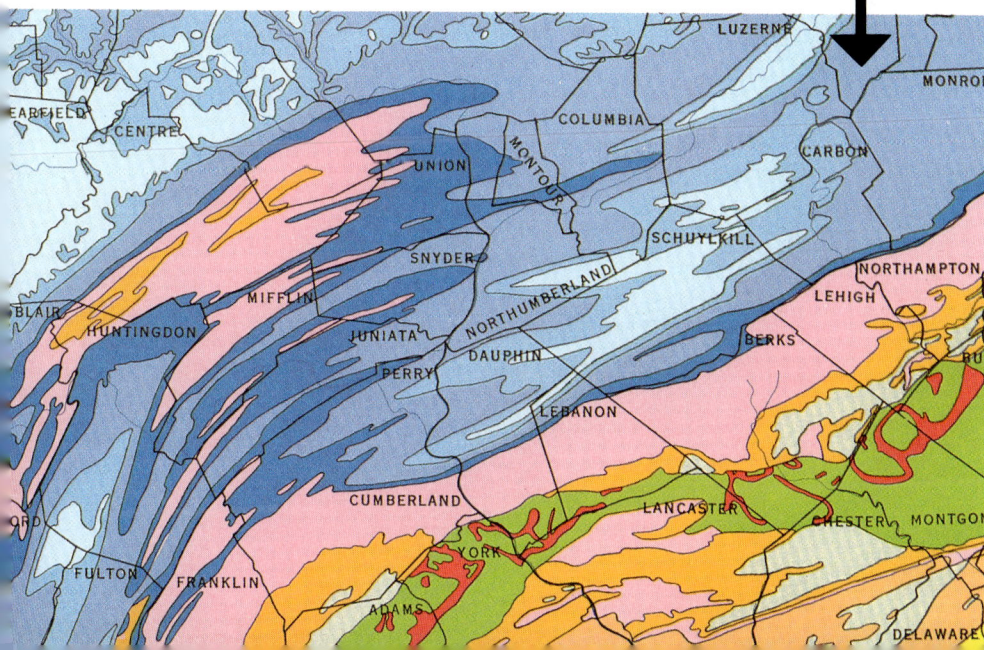

Conventional signs

Great Britain

Electricity transmission line (with pylons spaced conventionally)	Radio or TV mast
Pipe line (arrow indicates direction of flow)	Church — with tower / or — with spire
ruin — Buildings	Chapel — without tower or spire
Public buildings (selected)	Chimney or tower
Quarry	Glasshouse
Spoil heap, refuse tip or dump	Graticule intersections at 5' intervals
Coniferous wood	Heliport
Non-coniferous wood	Triangulation pillar
Mixed wood	Windmill with or without sails
Orchard	Windpump
	Park or ornamental grounds

TOURIST INFORMATION

Parking		
Picnic site	Youth hostel	Public telephone
Camp site	Golf course or links	Motoring organisation telephone
Caravan site	Bus or coach station	Public convenience (in rural areas)

United States

Sounding—Depth curve	Marsh (swamp)
Dry lake bed	Inundated area
Woodland	Mangrove
Submerged marsh	Scrub
Orchard	Wooded marsh
Vineyard	Bldg. omission area

France

Équipements - Environnement

Voie ferrée, station	Pétrole ou gaz naturel	Église ou chapelle
Tramway	Carrière	Cimetière · Calvaire
Altiport	Mine	Château
Aérodrome	Transporteur aérien	Fort
Aéroport	Usine	Ruines
Tour ou pylône de télécommunications	Barrage	Monument
Borne d'appel d'urgence	Phare ou balise	Grotte
Frontière	Moulin à vent	Maison forestière
Bureau de douane	Château d'eau	Forêt ou bois
	Établissement hospitalier	Forêt domaniale

Most maps have a list of conventional signs printed in the margin for easy reference. These charts show different symbols used in various countries.

On large-scale maps the features can be shown in their correct shape, size and position. On smaller-scale maps the features have to be simplified to make the map clearer. Special symbols called **conventional signs** are used to represent the features on the map.

Roads, railways and rivers are shown in different colours and widths according to their importance. On these pages are some examples of conventional signs that appear on maps. These signs are very useful, as they show what to expect or to look out for even before visiting an area. Look at this map of a small town and write down some of the things that you would see if you went there.

What is the red triangle?

What is the red dot?

Make a list of the conventional signs that you can find on a map of your area (and compare your list with the one shown opposite).

You could design your own conventional signs. What would you choose for a school, a hospital, a zoo and a fire station?

Conventional signs are now used in many different ways. Can you recognize the three shown below? You may see them marked on the doors of buildings.

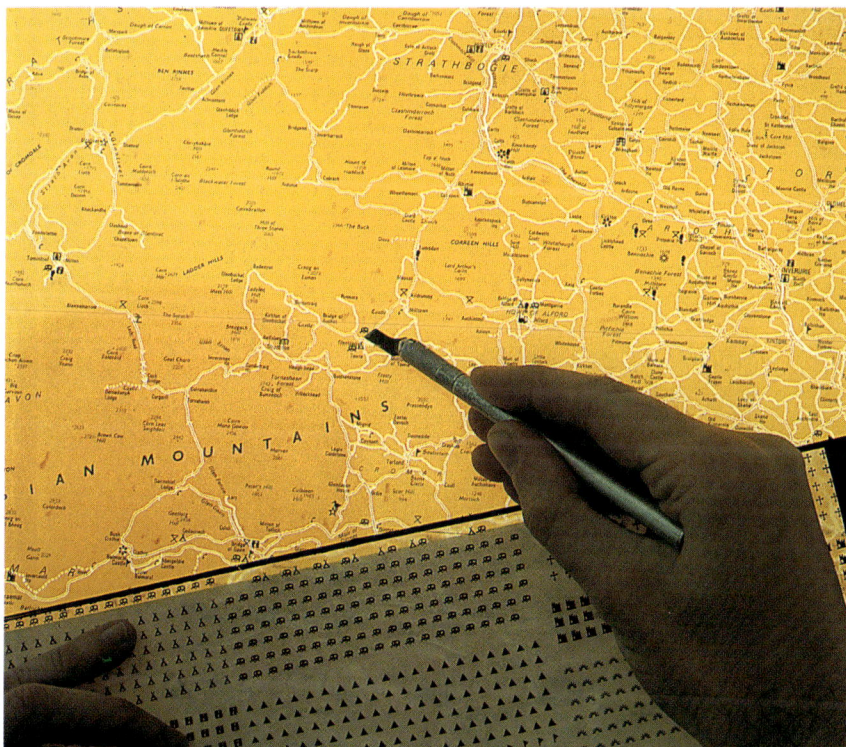

Above: Once you become familiar with symbols you can quickly locate many features, from bus stations to picnic sites.

The cartographer selects the symbols from a printed sheet and sticks them down on to the map in the appropriate place. A wax adhesive on the back of the sheet is used for fixing them in place.

Grid references

A **grid** is a series of lines superimposed on a map. It provides a convenient reference system with which to locate a place to which you may be travelling or items of particular interest.

Many countries have their own **national grid** which covers the whole of that country and is printed on all its maps.

The lines of latitude and longitude on a globe form a grid, but they are not as easy to use as a rectangular grid. Different countries use slightly different types of grid, and instructions on how to use the particular grid are usually printed along the margin of the map.

First, the country is divided into squares. The squares are identified by numbers or letters. Using the grid squares it is possible to give a grid reference which will locate any point on the map. For example, on the map shown here, the High road can be found in square D8.

	square	page
High Oaks	W 18	141
High road	D 8	45
High street	N 12	96
High timber	Z 3	21
High trees	S 4	21
High view ave.	P 17	14

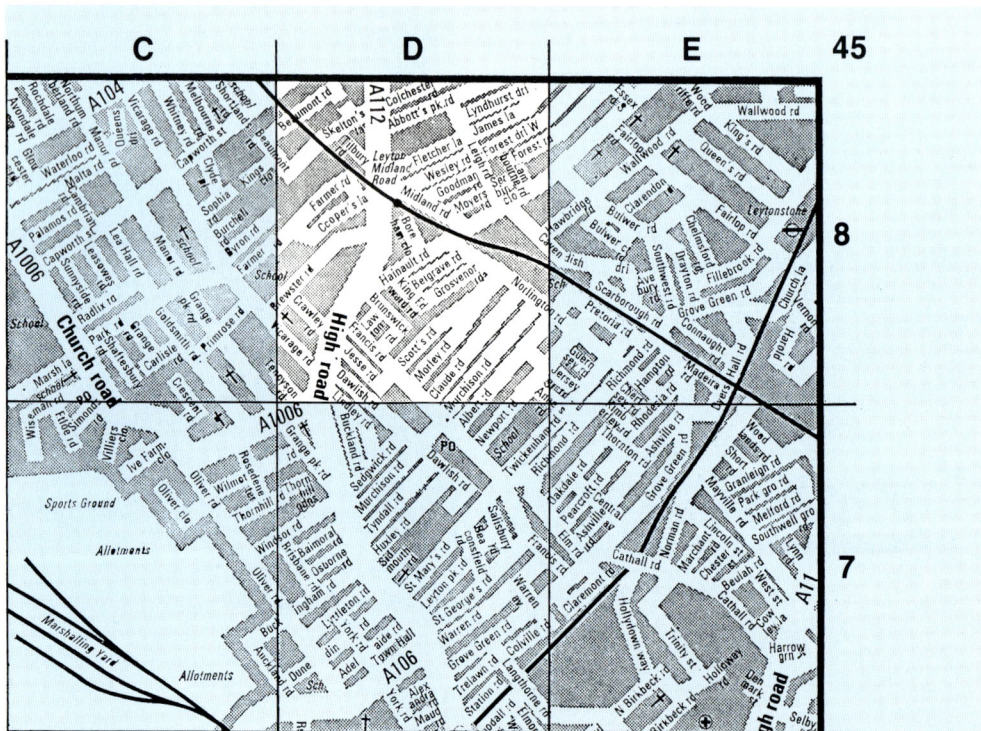

The letter and number reference system above will help you to locate any road on the map. Some roads extend into two grid squares and you could give a reference for each end of the road. Practise giving references to features and spotting them on the map. Remember that each reference on this map will have a letter and a number.

Archaeologists excavating a site use a grid system to record the exact place in which they find the artefacts discovered during the dig. This allows them to analyse the site long after the remains have been removed.

This 1:50,000 scale map has grid lines spaced at distances representing 1 kilometre on the ground (at this scale the lines are 2cm apart on the map). The vertical lines are numbered in kilometres east. The horizontal lines are numbered in kilometres north.

With this type of grid a more precise reference can be given. First choose a point on the map, and using the vertical lines which are numbered along the bottom you can estimate the distance eastwards. This distance is called the **Eastings**. Using the horizontal grid lines numbered up the side of the map, estimate the distance northwards, called **Northings**. Divide the space between the grid lines by eye into ten imaginary divisions, to give a more accurate reference.

The full reference comprises two sets of numbers, Eastings and Northings. The Eastings always come before the Northings.

References are usually provided in this form, with the Eastings read along the bottom of the map, followed by the Northings read up the side of the map.

If you have difficulty in remembering, say 'along the hall and up the stairs'.

With geographical co-ordinates the latitude is given before the longitude. For example:

Latitude 39°13′26″ North, Longitude 98°32′30″ West.

Check the reference instructions on the margin of the map that you are using.

If you wanted to meet someone at the camp site marked on the map, you could give them a grid reference. The diagram explains how you can pinpoint the exact location.

Meet us at
074 155
on Wednesday
from
Janet

Len and Linda
45 Letsby Ave.
YORK

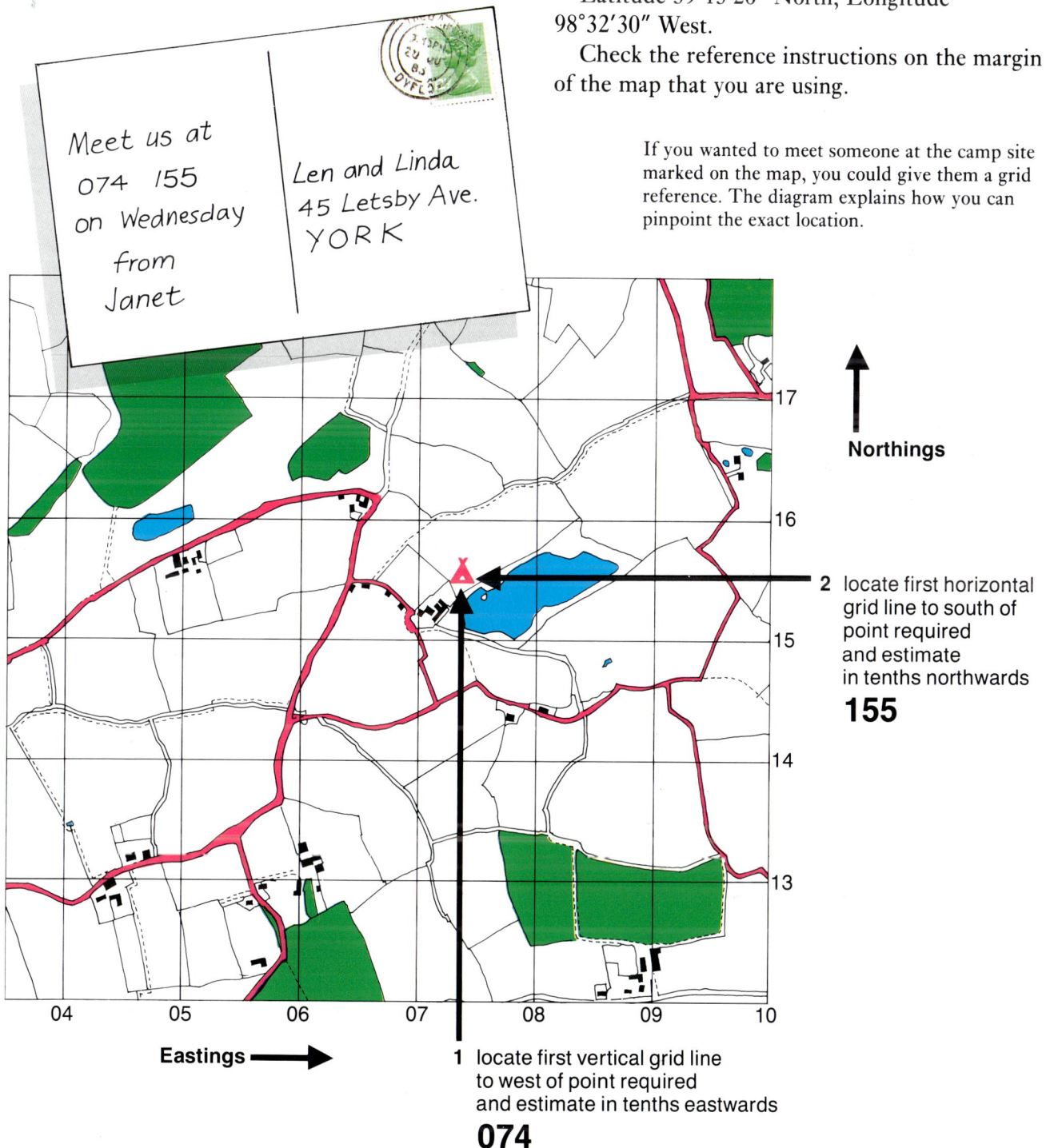

Northings

2 locate first horizontal
grid line to south of
point required
and estimate
in tenths northwards
155

Eastings ➡

1 locate first vertical grid line
to west of point required
and estimate in tenths eastwards
074

Early map makers

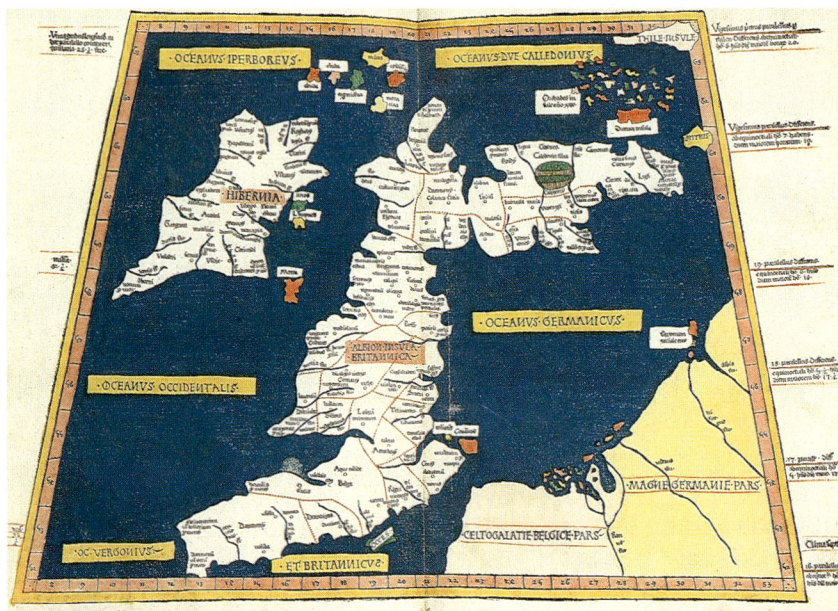

Above: Although early maps may not have been as accurate as modern ones, some of them were remarkably good attempts at portraying the shapes of countries, as the world map by Ptolemy shows.

The Roman map of Britain is marred by the fact that Scotland has been turned to the east — but it could still be used to navigate. We do not know exactly how these maps were surveyed, but clearly, observation of the stars played an important part.

The earliest known maps were made by the Babylonians and the Egyptians, some five thousand years ago. Only two or three of them have survived. The first Greek representation of the world was by the great astronomer and geographer Claudius Ptolemaeus or Ptolemy (AD87-150). He provided detailed instructions on how to draw maps, and in the 13th Century his work was rediscovered and copied in manuscript form. Two hundred years later, when woodcut and copper plate printing were introduced, his maps were published and distributed throughout Europe.

The end of the Middle Ages saw the beginning of the Age of Discovery, when the navigators of England, Portugal, Holland and Spain went out into unknown lands. From the charts and drawings which they brought back, detailed maps were printed. Cartographers often embellished the maps with heraldic devices and fanciful drawings of sea creatures.

In 1570 the first atlas of the world was published by the Flemish astronomer and geographer Abraham Ortelius. In 1579 the first atlas of the counties of England and Wales was published by William Saxton. As well as showing geographical features, his maps, and those of Humphrey Lloyd, another distinguished surveyor, included conventional signs (churches, castles, etc). Their surveys were made with very simple equipment, such as a **plane table**, a drawing board mounted on a tripod.

Another famous 17th-century mapmaker, John Ogilvy, produced **strip maps** describing the routes between large towns and cities. They proved very helpful to stage coach travellers who had difficulty in finding their way along the poor tracks which served as roads in those days. Ogilvy's maps were the forerunners of modern road and highway maps.

After the Scottish Rebellion of 1745 the Duke of Cumberland gave orders for Scotland to be mapped at a scale of 1 inch to 1000 yards. The task was carried out by a civilian quartermaster and notable mapmaker, William Roy, later General Roy.

Roy, who produced the first really accurate maps of Britain, suggested the formation of a National Survey, but it was not until the year after his death that his scheme was realized. In 1791 the Ordnance Survey, a national mapping organization, was formed and housed in the Tower of London. Their first production was a map of Kent, at a scale of 1 inch to 1 mile, published in 1801.

Not long afterwards (1804), Meriwether Lewis and William Clark, commissioned by President Jefferson, set off on their momentous two-year journey of exploration across America, from St Louis in the Mid West to the Pacific coast. The maps which they compiled were drawn with the help of trappers and traders.

In 1807 the US Department of the Treasury commissioned a Swiss scientist, Ferdinand Rudolf Hassler, to direct a survey of the entire coast of the United States. Hassler became the first Director of the U.S. Coast and Geodetic Survey, now called the National Ocean Survey.

The need for geological data resulted in the formation of the US Geological Survey in 1879.

The early cartographers decorated their maps with drawings of ships, sea monsters, battle scenes and other interesting features.

Many maps were made by explorers and pioneers such as Lewis and Clark, recording the topographic details as they travelled. The results have provided valuable sources of reference for those who followed.

Surveying

Early maps, produced with simple equipment, were generally little better than good sketch maps. Modern maps are much more accurate, and great care is taken to make sure that every feature is in its correct place.

To achieve this accuracy, mapmakers plot out the area which they are covering in a series of triangles. The triangles on the map are drawn to scale with those which have been selected in the actual area covered, and which have been permanently denoted by concrete or stone pillars called **triangulation** or 'trig' points. Some are marked with brass or bronze markers known as 'monuments'.

In Great Britain there are over 25,000 trig points. Many of them are on hill tops, others are circular brass markers ($2'' \times \frac{1}{2}''$) set into the roofs of high buildings. They are positioned so that they can be seen from other stations, and the angles of the triangles can then be measured.

One side of one of the triangles is measured very accurately, forming a **base** from which the co-ordinates (Eastings and Northings or latitude and longitude) of all the trig points can be mathematically computed. The trigs can then be plotted on a grid.

British Ordnance Surveyors occupy a triangulation station to measure the angles to other trig points in the area. The pillars are permanent marks of national scientific importance used as a basis for the complete survey of a country.

This triangulation survey of Long Island Sound was made by F R Hassler at the begining of the 19th Century as part of the US Coast Survey. It illustrates the principles of triangulation which have been used throughout the world.

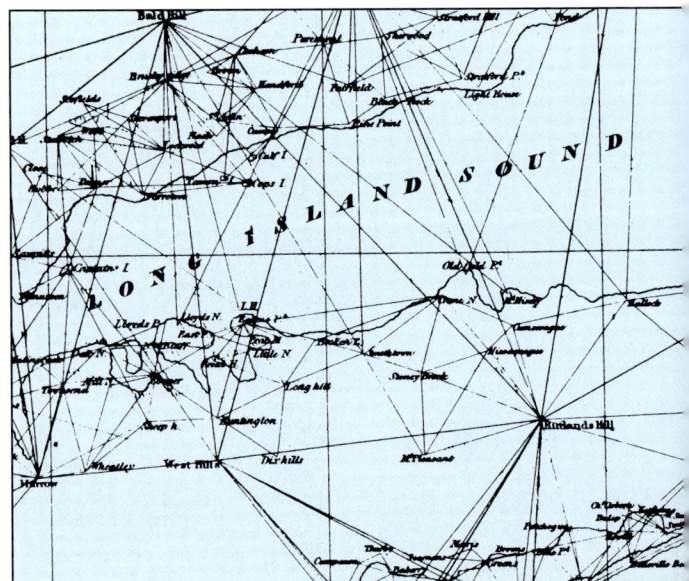

Using the **base measurement** and the angles of the triangles, the positions of the points needed to control the survey can be calculated. This system of measurement and calculation, called triangulation, was developed because in the past it was easy to measure angles, but difficult to measure distances, accurately. Nowadays distances are easily measured with electronic equipment, and surveyors tend to measure the sides of the triangles, rather than the angles. This method is called **trilateration**.

It is now also possible to calculate the co-ordinates of the trig points using equipment which receives signals from satellites in orbit around the earth. Once the co-ordinates of the control points have been calculated, the map detail within the triangles can be filled in.

Modern survey equipment can be used to measure to the tops of the highest buildings in a matter of seconds. This surveyor is recording the angle and distance to the top of an apartment block.

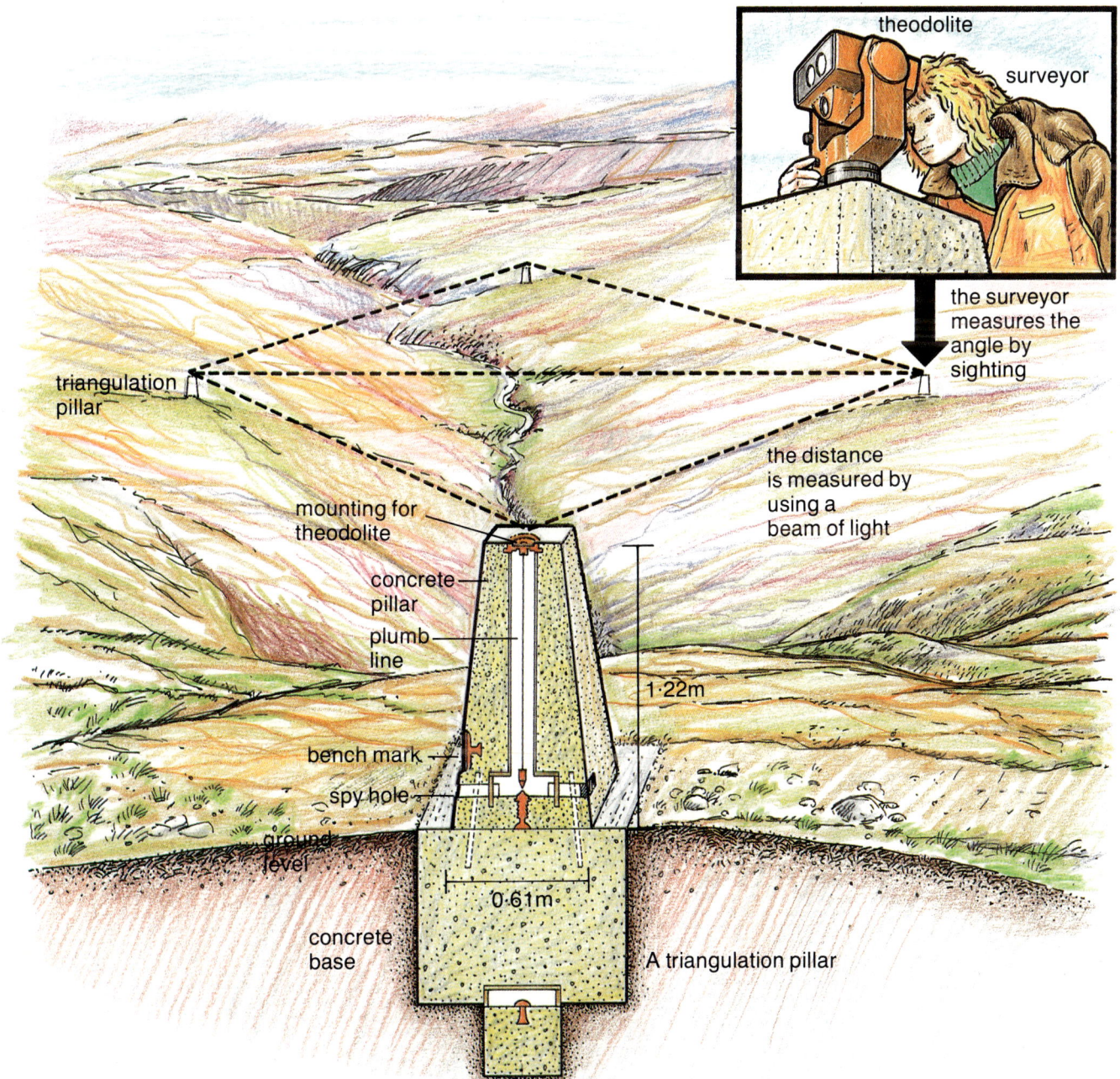

theodolite

surveyor

the surveyor measures the angle by sighting

triangulation pillar

the distance is measured by using a beam of light

mounting for theodolite

concrete pillar

plumb line

1·22m

bench mark

spy hole

ground level

0·61m

concrete base

A triangulation pillar

The tools for the job

The instrument used by a surveyor to measure angles is called a **theodolite**. It consists of a telescope attached to two circular protractors, one measuring horizontal angles and the other measuring vertical angles. On older instruments it was possible to see the angles marked on the circles, but on modern instruments the protractors are encased and viewed through microscopes. Sometimes the angles are shown on a **digital display**.

This surveyor in 18th-century uniform is using an early theodolite made in 1795 by Jesse Ramsden, a distinguished English instrument maker whose instruments were in great demand throughout Europe. The telescope and protractors can be seen clearly. Special machines were used to divide the circle into degrees, minutes and seconds and microscopes were used to obtain the most accurate observations.

A modern instrument, below, used for a motorway survey, is much more compact. As well as reading the angles, this instrument can be used to measure distances electronically.

The distance is displayed on a digital readout, or recorded directly on to magnetic tape to be entered later into a computer.

The theodolite can be placed on a **trig pillar** or on a tripod. The surveyor looks through the telescope and focusses on a target, lining it up with a cross in the telescope eyepiece. By viewing successive targets and noting their directions he can calculate the angles between them.

Some theodolites also measure distances by recording the time that it takes for a beam of light to leave the theodolite, hit the target and return. Based on the speed of light, it is possible to calculate the distances very accurately.

Other electronic distance measuring instruments use radio waves or laser beams. For example, **Doppler receivers** locate positions by measuring the frequency of radio waves transmitted from space satellites circling the earth.

As well as these modern instruments, surveyors use simple items of equipment such as tape measures, sighting rods, prismatic compasses and plane table boards, all of which have been in use for many centuries.

A simple survey can be carried out by measuring angles and distances from a central point to various features on a map and plotting them with a protractor.

Completing the map

The surveyor collects as much map information as possible with his instruments, using the **angle and distance method**, and fills in the detail between the triangulation points.

To complete the survey he uses a tape measure, plotting his measurements with a ruler and pencil.

Even when all the features – roads, buildings, rivers, etc. – have been plotted, there is still much to do. An important part of mapmaking is the collecting of additional information about the environment, details of the vegetation, whether trees are coniferous or deciduous, which areas are marsh or bog, whether the coastline is sand, mud or shingle, etc.

Names and descriptions all add to the value of the map. Local people are interviewed to make sure that the correct local names are used. Tourist information such as camp sites, wildlife parks, beaches and picnic sites are all added to the surveyor's working sheet.

A surveyor has to record information carefully and clearly so that the cartographer can understand his work and produce a map which everyone can read.

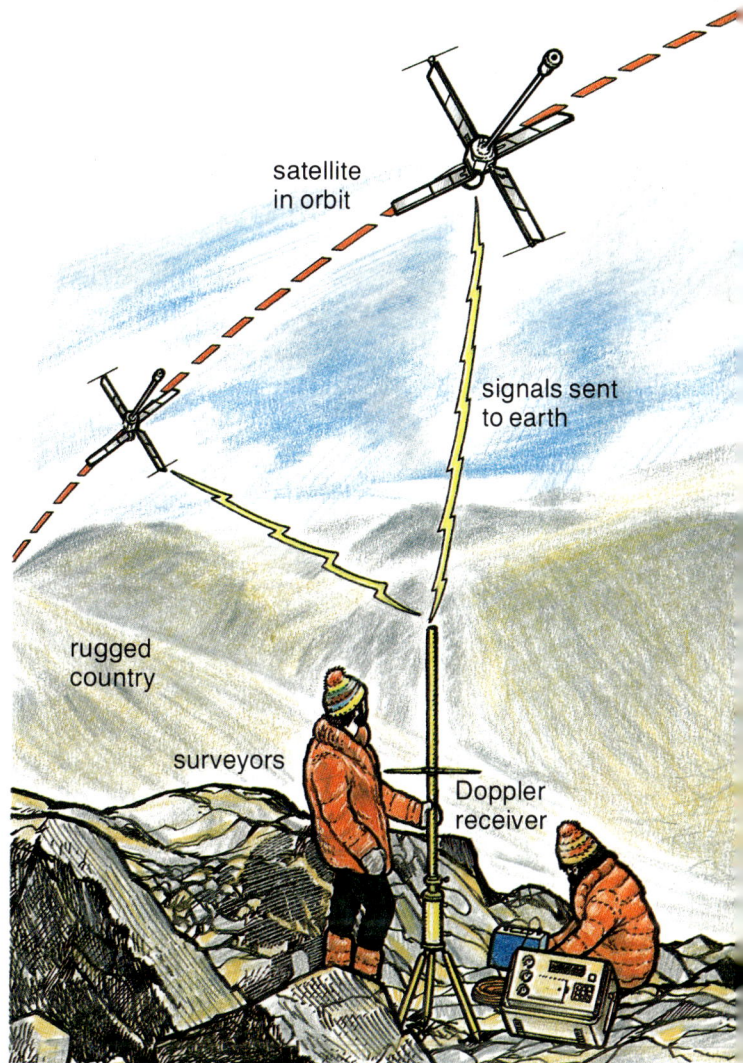

Surveyors taking Doppler measurements record the frequency shift of radio signals from a satellite. The signals will be used to calculate the latitude and longitude of the ground tracking station.

Once the positions of the control points have been established, the rest of the map information can be filled in. Using his sketching case and tape measure, the surveyor quickly completes the map and records the names of the features.

19

Measuring heights

A map printed on paper is flat, but if it is to represent accurately the three-dimensional world around us it must show the variations in ground heights, or **relief**. Cartographers have developed a number of different ways of depicting height.

Early mapmakers showed mountains and hills by a conventional sign: a simple drawing of a hill. In the 18th and 19th Centuries, military mapmakers wanted more detail, so they used a method of shading called **hachuring**. This has developed into the more sophisticated **hill-shading** used on some maps today. If you hold a hill-shaded map away from you, the hills seem to stand out from the valleys. However, although this method shows the general lie of the land, it does not tell you the actual height of the hills.

A successful method of showing height or relief is by varying the colours on the map according to the height of the ground above sea level. This is called **layer-tinting**: for example, the lowland areas are dark green, and as the land rises the colours change through brown to white in the highest areas. Since the vegetation in a valley is generally green and a mountain top is often covered in snow, this seems to be a good way of showing height variation.

In the 16th Century, William Saxton used conventional signs to show mountains and hills on his county maps. The symbol did not bear any resemblance to the mountain, but it provided general guidance.

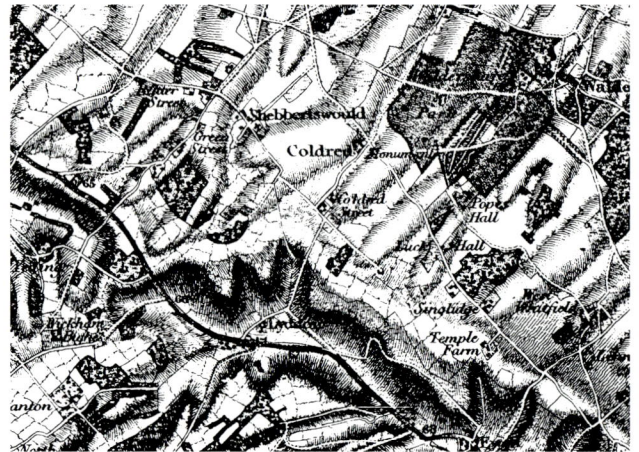

The hachuring used on this Ordnance Survey map published in 1801 gives a much more realistic view of the ground. Ridges and valleys can be clearly recognized.

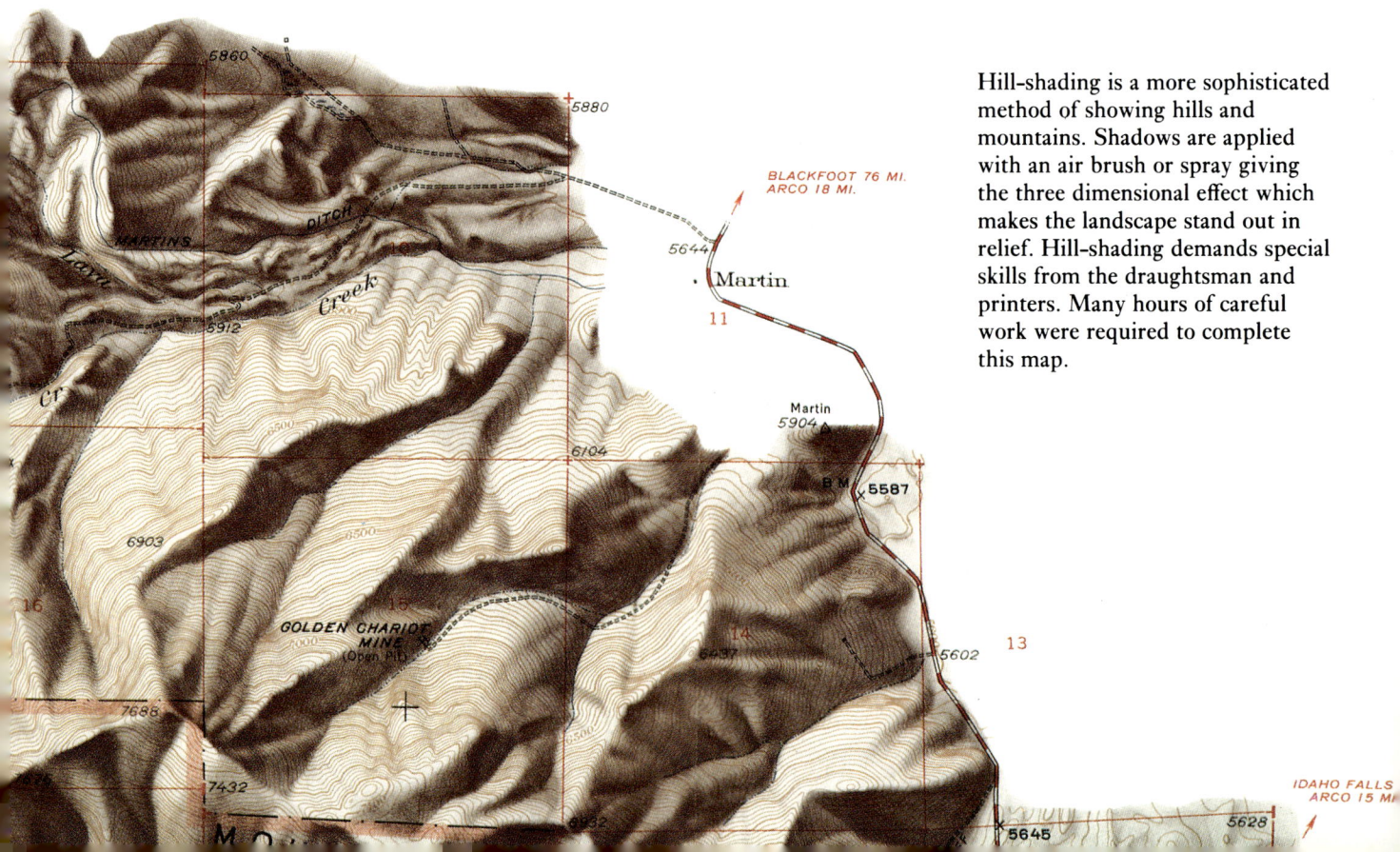

Hill-shading is a more sophisticated method of showing hills and mountains. Shadows are applied with an air brush or spray giving the three dimensional effect which makes the landscape stand out in relief. Hill-shading demands special skills from the draughtsman and printers. Many hours of careful work were required to complete this map.

Hill shading and layer tinting are generally supplemented by **spot heights**, which give the exact height of particular points on the map, either in feet or in metres above sea level.

Surveyors calculate differences in height by a method of **spirit-levelling**. The reference marks used, arrow-shaped and known as '**bench marks**', are chiselled into walls, buildings and bridges. In Great Britain, there are more than 500,000 bench marks, and for each of them the exact height above sea level has been recorded. In the United States a network of bronze monument bench marks can be found in a variety of places, from mountain tops to city sidewalks. Bench marks are used by engineers, architects and other surveyors for checking heights.

Another important way in which cartographers indicate land rising above or falling below sea level is by the use of **contours**: lines on the map joining points of the same height.

If the slope is steep, the distances between the contours on the map are narrow. If it is gradual, they are wide. By studying the contours carefully you can not only work out, for example, the height of a hill, but can also tell whether it will be easy or difficult to climb.

The surveyor is using a spirit level to measure the differences in height between two points on the ground. By adding or subtracting differences from known heights, new spot heights can be calculated.

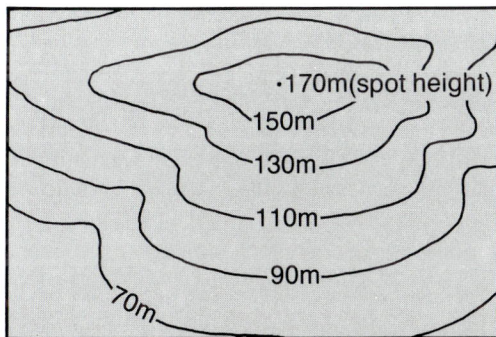

·170m(spot height)
150m
130m
110m
90m
70m

The illustration here shows how contours would look if drawn round a hillside at various heights above sea level. The map (left) shows how they would look from above and how it is possible to read off the heights of various features.

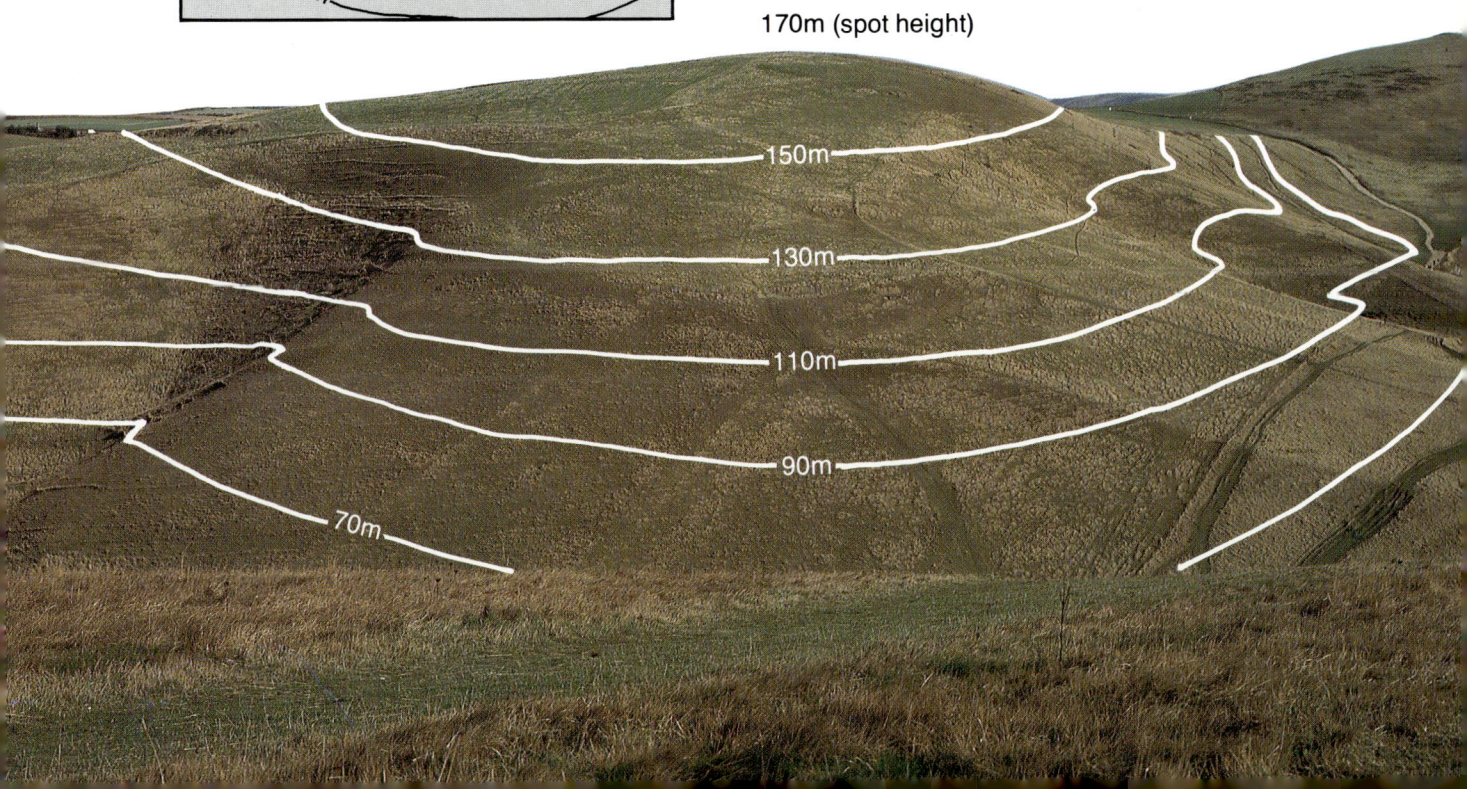

170m (spot height)
150m
130m
110m
90m
70m

Surveying from the air

The first successful aerial surveys were made from balloons during the American Civil War (1861-1865), when army engineers used bird's eye photographs to plot the movements of enemy troops on the ground. Since that time, the development of aviation and of camera technology has brought great advantages in **photogrammetry**, or mapmaking from aerial photographs.

With a specially designed camera, fitted into the floor of an aircraft and directed towards the ground, the air surveyor takes a series of film strips. When these have been developed and printed, the photographs are laid out to form an aerial view of a particular stretch of urban or rural landscape. The photographs are arranged to overlap each other, so that every point on the ground is covered by at least two photographs.

If the ground is very flat, details of roads, buildings and other features can be traced off the photographs. This method is often used for revising maps which have become out of date. The photographs may be enlarged or reduced to the same scale as the map.

Strips of overlapping aerial photographs are being laid out to provide photocover of the area being mapped. When the photographs are placed in the stereo-plotting machine opposite, a three-dimensional view of the ground can be seen. The operator then measures the features on the photographs.

If the area is mountainous or very hilly, a different technique has to be applied. When the overlapping photographs are viewed through a **stereoscope**, a three-dimensional view of the ground is provided. Specially designed plotting instruments are used to view the photograph as though it were a model, to measure the 3D picture, and to plot the map information directly on to paper or film.

From the 'model', contours can be drawn very quickly and accurately. The triangulation stations and other control points are used to obtain the correct scale and **orientation** for the aerial survey. The triangulation stations may be painted white, so that they can be seen clearly on the photographs.

When the aerial survey is complete, a surveyor takes the map out into the actual area so that he can add the details which were hidden under trees, etc. He also notes the road names and other items which could not be seen on the photographs.

Aerial surveys help to produce better maps and to reduce the cost of mapmaking, as well as speeding up the work.

Satellites and manned vehicles orbiting in space send back pictures of the earth, using the latest remote sensing equipment. This information is of great benefit to mapmakers. As the quality of the images recorded by the sensors improves, more and more information will be gleaned from the satellite pictures. There will, however, always be a need to take measurements on the ground.

Above: The completed map of Pleshey can be compared with an aerial view. Most of the features visible on the photograph have been shown on the map, though some have been simplified to make them clearer. The map shows additional features which cannot be seen from above, and the names of the features have been carefully recorded.

Cartography and computers

The draughtsman here is drawing with pen and ink in the style which has been used for centuries.

Here the more modern method of scribing is being used to produce a very consistent line.

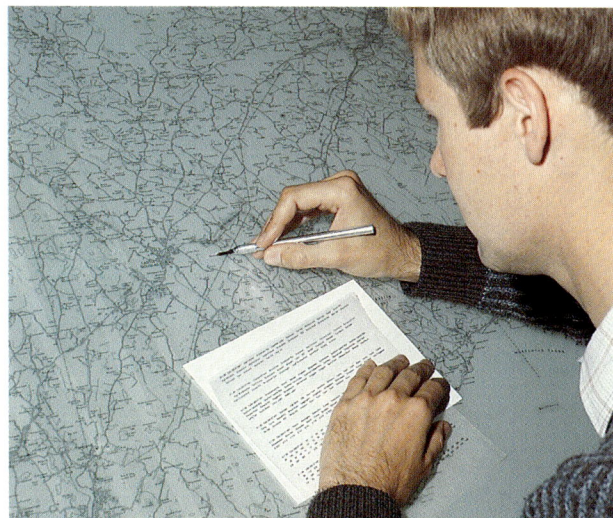

Names, house numbers and symbols are stuck down on wax-coated film.

When a survey is completed it is handed over to the **cartographers**. A draughtsman takes the surveyor's information and re-draws it, carefully selecting the information and presenting it in a clear and colourful way so that it will be both easy to read and attractive to the person using it. This requires great skill and patience. Special pens and inks are used, and a cartographer has to put in many hours of practice before becoming accomplished.

An alternative way of drawing the lines on a map is by **scribing,** in which the lines are cut away on a plastic-coated film, leaving a stencil of the map. Scribing produces very high quality cartography.

Names and conventional signs are printed on wax-coated film and are stuck down on to the map when the drawing is complete.

Nowadays much of a cartographer's work can be done with the help of computers, which as well as having the capacity to store large quantities of information can also be used for drawing maps.

As has already been explained, the grid reference of a point has two sets of numbers, denoting horizontal and vertical measurements on the map. Together these sets of numbers are known as the **co-ordinates** of the point. Each point on a map can be expressed (in numbers) as a set of co-ordinates, which can be stored in a computer memory bank. It is by this process that maps are **digitized**.

The completed map is laid on a table which contains a fine mesh of electronic wires. When a **cursor** is placed on the map, at the press of a button the computer can automatically record the co-ordinates of the point at the centre of the cursor. By moving the cursor around, the draughtsman can record the co-ordinates of every point on the map directly into the computer. He can also tell the computer what a particular feature is – for example, a building, a road, or a river. Names can be typed in, using the computer terminal keyboard.

When the map has been digitized and processed it is displayed on a Visual Display Unit (VDU) screen. Using the computer terminal, the data can be revised, by adding more information, removing unwanted information, and moving features about on the screen. The computer can

then be commanded to draw the map on an automatic plotting machine, which works a great deal faster than a cartographer can draw by hand. The pen on the plotting machine moves at more than 100 centimetres (40 inches) per second.

The draughtswoman is digitizing the features on the map by recording the co-ordinates of every point. Names are typed on the keyboard together with a description of the kind of feature being recorded.

The plotter can be commanded to draw the map quickly at any chosen scale.

When heights and contours have been digitized, a computer model of the ground can be drawn or viewed on the screen.

The model can be scaled, rotated and stretched in any direction.

surveying

drawing and adding the names

photographing

Printing and publishing

When the draughtsman has drawn or digitized the map, it is ready to be printed, but before the printing plates can be made, the map must first be photographed with a camera specially designed for this work. It may be as large as 7 metres (23ft) long and 2m (6½ft) wide, and will enlarge or reduce a drawing to any size, depending on the scale required.

The negative produced on the camera is placed in front of a **printing plate**, which has been treated with light-sensitive coating. When light passes through the negative it hardens the coating, leaving an image on the map on the plate. The image is then inked up, and the plate is ready to be used for printing.

Early printing presses were hand operated. The printing plates and a sheet of paper were placed flat on the bed of the press, and pressure was applied by means of a screw press. Today the flat-bed printing process most commonly used is known as '**off-set**', as the image is taken from the printing plate on to a rubber roller and then transferred to the paper. The roller saves wear and tear on the plate, so that more copies can be made before the plate will have to be replaced.

When large numbers of maps are required, a **rotary press**, which can print more than 10,000 per hour, is used. In this process the printing plate is fixed round a cylinder. The image is transferred from the cylinder to a rubber roller and then on to the paper.

To obtain the full range of colours required for a map, the four primary colours – black, red, blue and yellow – are used. All other colours can be

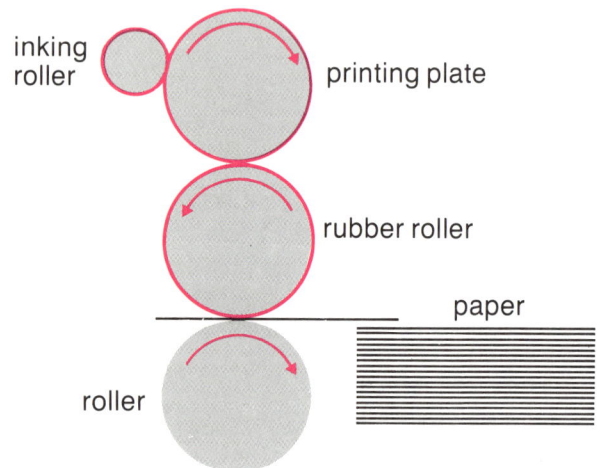

A rotary printing machine which transfers the inked image to the paper by means of a rubber roller.

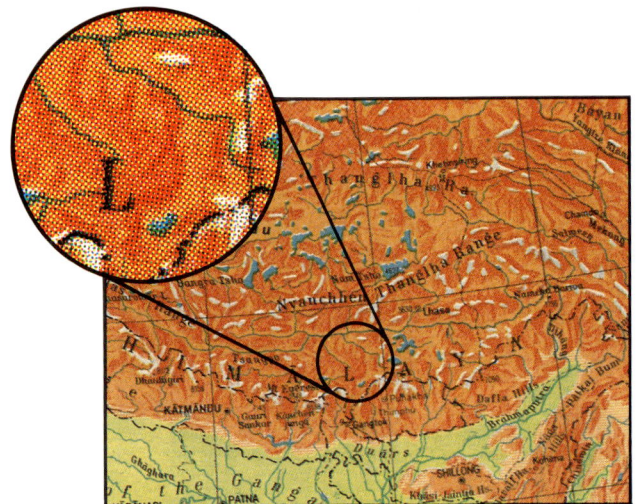

This enlarged view of the image shows how a range of colours can be formed by mixing the primary colours.

making printing plates

printing

folding, binding and transporting

produced by mixing these four. The strength of colour is varied by **screening**, or printing the image in dots of different sizes. If you look at a map through a microscope you will see that some colours are pure, but that orange, for example, is made by printing red dots on yellow, and green by printing blue dots on yellow. The printers must exercize great skill to register the colours exactly and to make sure that the place names, conventional signs, numbers, etc., are sharply and accurately defined.

In this rapidly changing world, no map remains accurate for long. Old buildings are demolished and new ones constructed; airports are extended; new roads and highways are built; man-made lakes are created. Maps constantly need revision, and teams of surveyors go out every day to record the changes on their master survey drawings. When the new information has been checked and verified it is handed over to the cartographers, who redraw or digitize a map where necessary. A new edition is then printed and published.

Rotary printing machines like this can print four-colour maps at speeds of 10,000 maps per hour. Great skill and patience are required in setting the plates to give the correct register.

Make your own map

You can easily make a map yourself, using simple
equipment: a prismatic compass, a tape measure,
two poles, some paper and a board or small table
on which to pin it. (A rubber may also be useful
in case you make mistakes.)

A prismatic compass enables
you to sight an object and read
its bearing at the same time

A radial map

1 To map a small area – such as the land
   around your home – choose and mark a
   reference point in the centre of it, from which
   you can see the whole area.

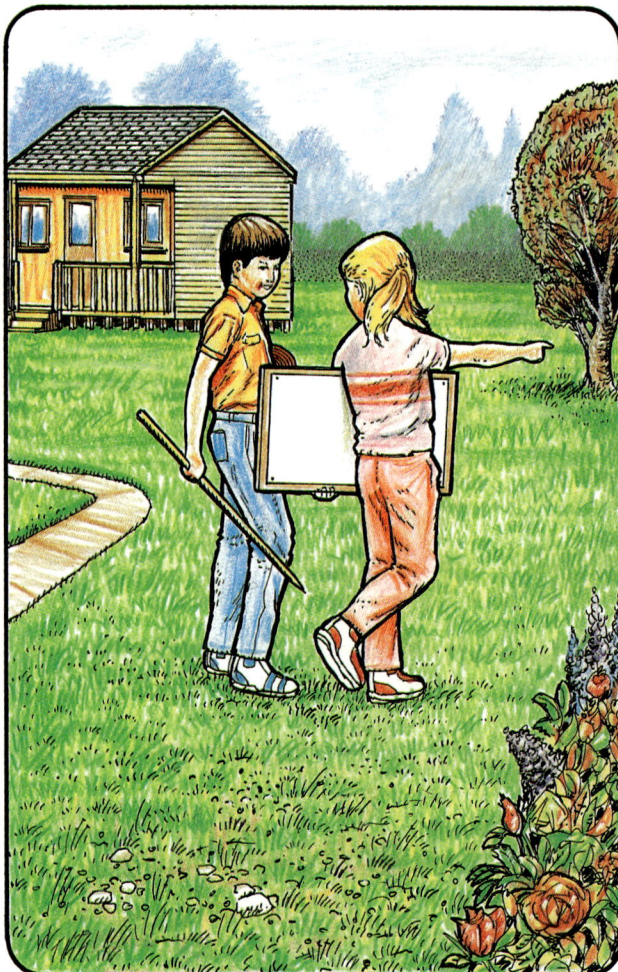

2 Pace out the approximate length of the area,
   and select a suitable scale which will enable
   you to plot the map on the paper.

3 Stand on the reference point and use the
   compass to find north. Mark a point on the
   paper to represent your position, and draw an
   arrow to represent north.

4 With the compass, take radial bearings (angles from north in a clockwise direction) to the points that you have chosen to map. With the protractor, draw the bearings on the map.

5 Now measure from the reference point to the map features, and plot the distances to scale along the bearings on the map. Hold the tape measure horizontally as you take the measurements.

6 You will soon have a series of dots representing the corners of buildings, paths, trees, etc. These can be joined up to form the map.

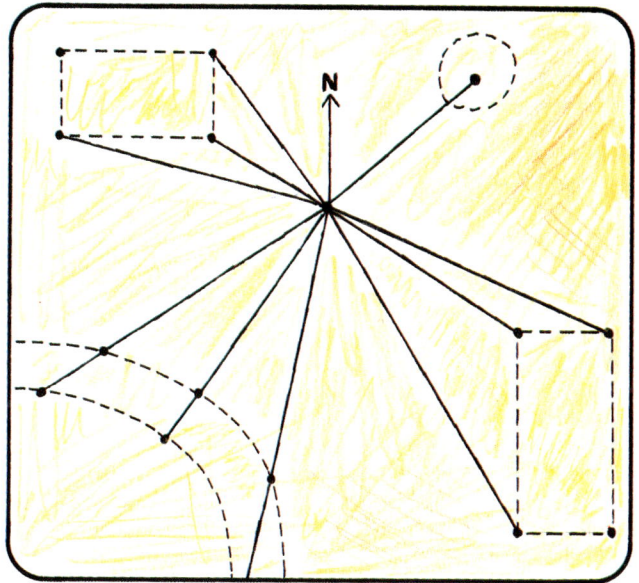

7 When you have finished, rub out the radial lines representing the bearings. Then ink in the detail and add the names and descriptions.

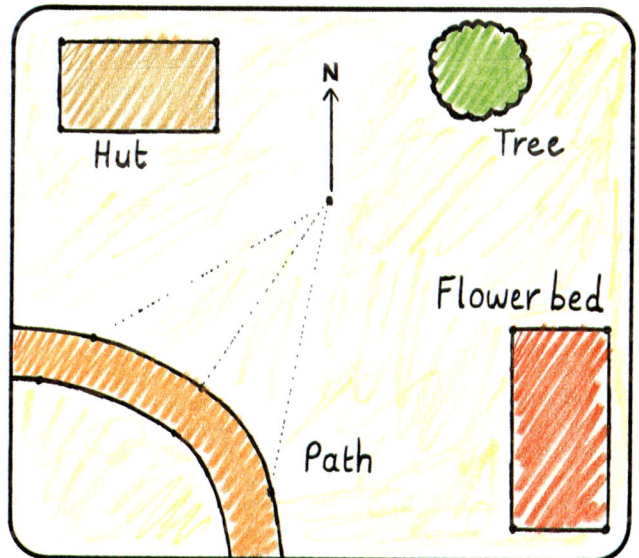

Making a larger survey

You can survey a larger area, say your school grounds, by creating a triangle from three intervisible points.

Measure the sides of the triangle ABC, and plot the triangle carefully with dividers. You now have three points from which you can take radial bearings and measurements.

Further triangles can be projected on the sides AB, BC and CA. Try to form triangles with sides as near equal as possible.

Don't forget to draw a grid and a scale and to add the title of the survey.

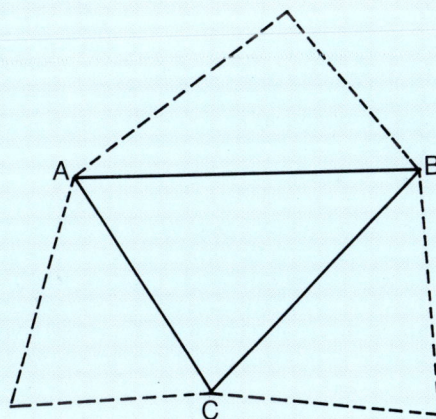

Maps of the future

The photographs taken from satellite sensors in outer space are continually improving in quality, and it will soon be possible to make very detailed maps from them.

Automobiles, trucks and trains will soon have their own mobile maps displayed on television screens in front of the driver. Map co-ordinates will be converted and relayed by voice synthesizers to describe the best routes. At the press of a button, distances will be selected, measured and described.

Video maps are already in use for recording data about electricity, telephone and water supply lines. Before long, maps will be available on small pocket television screens to guide mountain climbers and walkers.

These are just some of the many projects in which scientists and cartographers are applying their knowledge and skills to produce maps for the years beyond 2000.

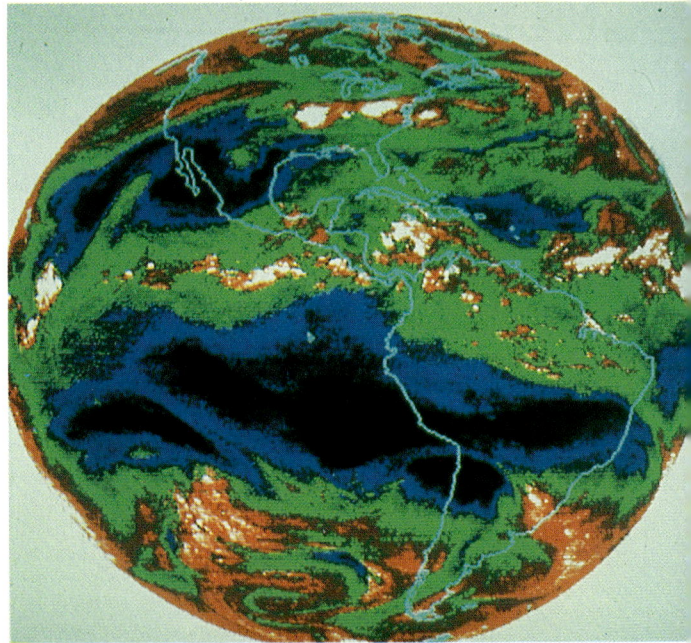

This satellite imagery maps the temperature and moisture profile of North and South America.

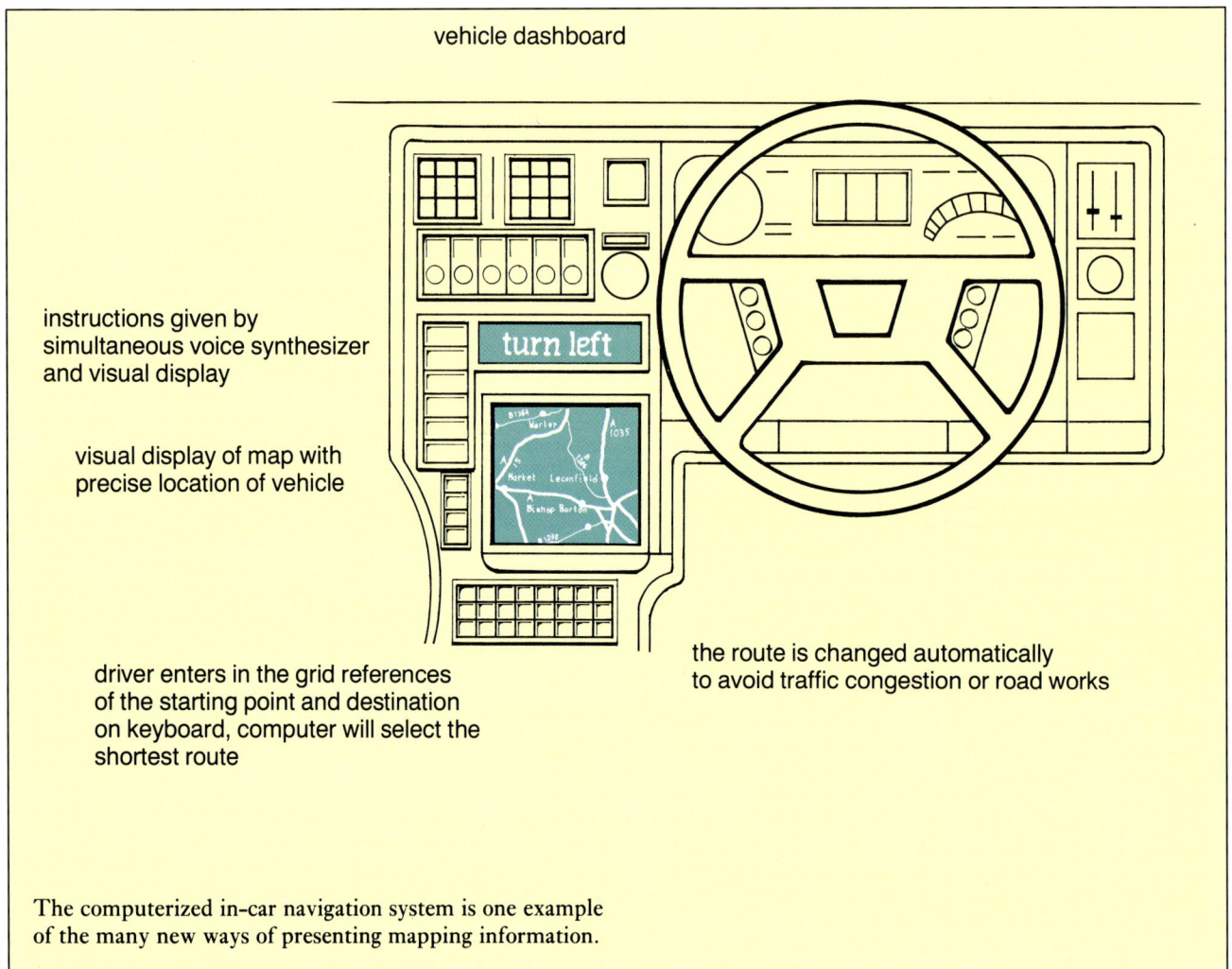

vehicle dashboard

instructions given by simultaneous voice synthesizer and visual display

turn left

visual display of map with precise location of vehicle

driver enters in the grid references of the starting point and destination on keyboard, computer will select the shortest route

the route is changed automatically to avoid traffic congestion or road works

The computerized in-car navigation system is one example of the many new ways of presenting mapping information.

Glossary

Angle and distance method   A method of locating a point by recording its direction and distance from a known point.

Base   An accurately measured distance used as a foundation for a triangulation.

Bench mark   A mark on a post, pillar or building of which the height has been accurately measured.

Cartography   Map drawing.

Contour   A line drawn on a map joining points of equal height.

Conventional signs   Symbols used to show different features on a map: e.g. roads, bridges, etc.

Co-ordinates   Distances measured parallel to the axes of a reference system.

Cursor   An index marker used for digitizing maps.

Digital display   An array of numbers displayed electronically.

Digitizing   The process of converting a map into numerical form to store it in a computer.

Doppler receiver   A survey instrument used for locating a ground position in relationship to satellites orbiting the Earth.

Double-diced scale   A scale line which shows measurements in miles, kilometres, or other units, at map scale.

Eastings   The distance to a point measured due East from the western edge of a map.

Equator   A line round the globe equidistant from the North and South Poles.

Geographic co-ordinates   Map references based on latitude and longitude.

Globe   A sphere or ball representing the Earth.

Hachuring   A method of line-shading used to depict hills or mountains.

Hillshading   A method of continuous tone-shading used on maps to give a 3-dimensional effect to hills and mountains.

Latitude   The distance North or South from the Equator.

Layer tinting   A method of colouring different levels to show variations of height above or below sea level.

Longitude   The distance East or West from the Greenwich Meridian.

Magnetic variation   The difference between the directions of the Magnetic Pole and the North Pole.

National Grid   A series of lines superimposed on a map to use as a reference system for a particular state or country.

Northings   The distance to a point measured due North from the Southern edge of a map.

Offset printing   Using a rubber roller to transfer the image from a printing plate on to paper.

Orientation   Correlating the map with the ground.

Photogrammetry   The science of taking measurements from photographs.

Plane table   A drawing board mounted on a tripod.

Projection   A method of presenting the curved surface of a globe on a plain piece of paper.

Relief   Variation in height and depth.

Representative fraction   The scale relationship between measurements on the map and on the ground.

Rotary press   A printing machine on which the printing plate is attached to a roller.

Scale   The ratio of reduction in the size of features shown on a map.

Screening   The method of mixing three colours to produce many different colours and shades.

Scribing   A method of drawing maps by cutting away lines on plastic-coated films to produce a stencil of the map.

Spirit level   An instrument that records differences in height, using a bubble in a tube of liquid.

Spot height   A point of known height printed on a map.

Stereoscope   An instrument which gives a 3-dimensional view from a pair of photographs taken from slightly different angles.

Strip maps   Maps which describe the narrow route of a road or river.

Surveying   Observing, measuring and recording information.

Theodolite   An instrument used for measuring horizontal and vertical angles.

Triangulation   A method of surveying based on the measurement of the angles of triangles.

Trig pillar   A stone or concrete monument marking a survey control point.

Trig point   A permanent survey mark at the corner of a triangle. Usually on a high point, a hill or high building.

Trilateration   A method of surveying based on the measurement of the lengths of the sides of triangles.

Index

Acknowledgements

Threshold Books and the publishers gratefully acknowledge the help given by the Ordnance Survey, Southampton.

Illustration Credits
Aerofilms 23; American Society for Photogrammetry and Remote Sensing 22 (top); British Airways 9 (top); British Library 14 (top); Crown Copyright 9 (bottom); Geoffrey Drury 3 (bottom), 4 (bottom), 11 (top), 21 (bottom); Ikon 15 (top); Institute of Archaeology: photo Peter Drewett 12 (bottom); London Zoo 2; Maanmittanshallitus, Helsinki 8 (top); The Manhattan Map Co. Inc 11 (bottom); Nicholsons 12 (top); Ordnance Survey 10 (top), 11 (bottom), 16 (bottom), 17 (top), 18, 19 (bottom), 20 (middle), 21 (top), 22 (bottom), 23 (bottom), 24, 25, 27. Royal Geographical Society 14 (bottom); Science Photo Library 4 (top), 30 (top); US Geological Survey 20 (bottom), 25 (bottom).

Diagrams and Drawings: Ray and Corrine Burrows 7 (top), 17, 19, 26–27 (top), 28, 29; Peter Dennis 9, 15; Robert Wheeler 5, 6, 7 (bottom), 8, 13, 26 (bottom), 30.

Picture research: Christine Vincent.

First published in 1987
by Faber and Faber Limited,
3 Queen Square, London WC1N 3AU

Typeset by August Filmsetting, Haydock, St Helens

Printed and bound in Italy by New Interlitho, Milan
All rights reserved

© Threshold Books Limited, 1987

The How It Is Made series was conceived, designed and produced
by Threshold Books Limited,
661 Fulham Road, London SW6 5PZ

General Editor: Barbara Cooper

British Library Cataloguing in Publication Data

Baynes, John
  Maps—(How It Is Made)
  1. Maps—Juvenile Literature
  1. Title   II. Series
  912   GA130
  ISBN 0–571–14732–1